BRITAIN IN OLD PH

AROUND
CHICHESTER

DAVID BATHURST

SUTTON PUBLISHING LIMITED

Sutton Publishing Limited
Phoenix Mill · Thrupp · Stroud
Gloucestershire · GL5 2BU

First published 1997

Reprinted in 2004

Copyright © David Bathurst, 1997

British Library Cataloguing in Publication Data
A catalogue record for this book is available from the
British Library.

ISBN 0-7509-1362-2

Typeset in 10/12 Perpetua.
Typesetting and origination by
Sutton Publishing Limited.
Printed in Great Britain by
J.H. Haynes & Co. Ltd, Sparkford.

The priory church at Boxgrove, regarded as one of the most important ecclesiastical buildings in West
Sussex.

CONTENTS

This early twentieth-century view of Bosham High Street gives little warning of the tourist invasion that was to come!

This selection of views of Chichester dates back to 1912, and gives an at-a-glance guide to Chichester's best known landmarks.

INTRODUCTION

This book is intended to offer the reader a selection of old photographs depicting not only the city of Chichester but also the surrounding villages. The site of modern Chichester has a long history. The Iron Age Regni tribe evidently chose a good site for their settlement, for when the Romans arrived they built their new town Noviomagus there. After the Romans departed, the town fell into ruins and the Saxon chieftain Aella gave the remains to his son Cissa, after whom it was named 'Cissa's Ceaster' (castle).

The Trundle, the best of many magnificent viewpoints within a short drive of the city, offers splendid views of the city and its compact community set amid fields, woods, salt marshes and harbour waters, the whole dominated by the thin cathedral spire, 277 feet high, pointing sword-like towards heaven. When one also considers its Roman wall, sixteenth-century market cross and Georgian architecture, it is easy to see why Chichester has been a magnet for visitors – and photographers – for many years.

Several of the villages surrounding Chichester have also attracted the photographer for a variety of reasons. Bosham's seductive charms, Boxgrove's monastic grandeur, Lavant's capricious waters and Tangmere's wartime pride have all provided wonderful subjects for both amateur and professional photographers.

The result is the easy availability of a vast number of photographs of Chichester and its surroundings in published form. When asked, therefore, to compile this book for Sutton Publishing's prestigious series 'Britain in Old Photographs', I decided that my starting point should be fresh and individual perspectives on city and village life. The best chance of achieving this was through the previously unpublished private collections of local residents. As a result, all but four of the photographs in this book come from private collections. Many of the views will be familiar ones, capturing the quintessence of the city and its surrounding communities, but also included are photographs depicting previously unpublished subjects.

The photographs themselves cover a very wide timespan: the earliest was taken in 1865 and the most recent in 1987. Many of the views are unrecognizable today, and would be impossible to capture on film again. Others, however, are reassuringly familiar and provide a welcome thread of stability in a world that seems to become more hectic every day.

I owe a huge debt of thanks to those who lent photographs to me (a list of acknowledgements is given at the back of the book) and can only speculate about the number of wonderful perspectives on the Chichester area that remain undisclosed and unpublished!

David Bathurst
January 1997

Bishop Durnford, who gave his name to a street in the Parklands area of Chichester, was Bishop of Chichester from 1870 to 1896. This drawing of his tomb is by George Fossick.

CHICHESTER

For most people the name Chichester excites images of gentility, gracefulness and good living; a pleasant place to come to shop, to stroll and to eat. It has the hallmarks of user-friendliness. The shopping area is paved; the Cross provides a natural meeting place; and for spiritual refreshment the Cathedral is never far away. Yet these cosy images fail to recognize the city's proud history as a community which has always worked hard and played hard, and whose businessmen have had to come to terms with ever-increasing social and economic change. However, although it would be wrong to present an image of Chichester as a changeless paradise, it would also be wrong to fail to recognize the perpetual 'picture-postcard' quality of its most cherished treasures.

Accordingly, the photographs in this section endeavour to reconcile the comfortable image of Chichester with the reality of workaday life in the city.

I start with the Cross, Chichester's central and focal point, and a number of pictures of the city's principal streets and particular buildings on those streets. There then follows a selection of Cathedral-based pictures before a group of photos representing all aspects of Chichester community life including transport, hospitals, factories, education and, on the lighter side, cricket and amateur operatics.

The Cross from West Street, *c.* 1900. On the left is the Anchor Hotel which in 1910 combined with the Dolphin Hotel next door to create The Dolphin & Anchor. The Dolphin Hotel contained a coaching yard and advertised 'excellent stabling and loose boxes'; at one time it served as the headquarters of the Automobile Club of Great Britain and Ireland, and of the Sussex County Automobile Club. The writing on the reverse of this postcard view no doubt expresses the sentiments of many present and past Cicestrians: 'This is a lovely place.'

A similar view photographed several decades later. The road sign is a reminder that all traffic between Portsmouth and Brighton would have had to negotiate the Cross. Imagine HGVs attempting the same thing today!

The Cross from East Street. Built in 1501 by Bishop Edward Story, it was originally the focus of a market-place; as Ian Nairn and Nikolaus Pevsner remarked, it was 'quite a setting for cabbages'. Some five hundred years later it is still a popular meeting place. On the right is Lennards' shoe shop. The pub on the left is the Royal Arms, known locally as the Old Punch House. It was built on the site of a house where Lord Lumley entertained Elizabeth I in 1591. In 1840 the landlord was appointed manufacturer of Chichester Milk Punch to Queen Victoria.

The Cross from East Street, 1892. This view of the Cross and Cathedral bell-tower is virtually unchanged more than a century later. The Cross, like the Cathedral, was built of Caen stone.

This reproduction of a colour postcard also shows the Cross from East Street. Note the ladies' hairdressers offering haircutting and shaving!

The Cross from South Street. In 1997 the site of the ladies' hairdressers was occupied by Bonus Print; snaps instead of snips one might say! The lantern on top of the Cross is octagonal in shape and was last altered in 1746.

The view from the Cross on a sunny day in 1930, looking east. In his *Visitors' Guide to Sussex*, Jim Cleland wrote that the Cross 'has been well used, to judge from the wearing of the stone seats, for generations', and described it as 'a gift of lasting enrichment to Chichester'. The seating is now especially popular with the young.

Bulls Ltd on the west side of North Street, 1920s. Specializing in china, hardware, glass, toys and fancy goods, Bulls Ltd had branches in Portsmouth, Havant and Southsea during this period.

The view up North Street, 1899. Today, only the 1731 Council building, with its impressive pillars and brick arches jutting across the pavement, is recognizable. The Assembly Room inside dates from 1783, and the 1794 guide to Chichester describes it as 'very elegant [and] spacious – honoured by the attendance of persons of the first rank'.

North Street photographed just a few years later than the previous picture. A solitary motor car hogs the centre of the road. The Market House, now known as the Butter Market, is just visible on the right; built by Nash in 1807 it replaced the Cross as central Chichester's market-place.

North Street, looking up towards Northgate, 1950s. On the right is the Church of St Peter the Less, which was demolished in 1957. It was replaced by a thoroughfare, appropriately called St Peter's, and a store, now Hoopers. The demolition was probably the result of low attendance and high running costs, as with many other redundant or demolished churches in Chichester.

The Singer sewing machine company's store stood on the west side of North Street close to Northgate. This photograph of the store was taken from Priory Road in the early 1960s.

The Northgate flats, 1960s. A nursing home had previously occupied this site; in 1997 the building houses a firm of estate agents, with a smart new shopping precinct immediately behind.

The fire at the premises of solicitors Thomas Eggar Verrall Bowles in South Street in 1987. Even in the relatively short period since this picture was taken, many of the shop fronts have changed, perhaps reflecting the ever-increasing pace of life.

South Street, probably in the 1930s. The church on the left is the Congregational Church, built in 1892 and demolished in 1980 following the decision of the Congregationalists to unite with the Methodists in a new building nearby. Work on the new church began in 1981 and it opened in August 1982.

An almost identical view taken in the 1950s. Note the Morris Minor and the subtle change to the Lewis logo on the extreme right.

This unusual building on the west side of Southgate was owned jointly by Stricklands Corn Merchants and B.J. Howard newsagents in the late 1960s. By 1972 it was owned solely by B.J. Howard. The petrol pumps belonged to Wadham's garage (out of picture to the right). The building was demolished in July 1973 and the site occupied by offices.

War Memorial
and St Pancras Church,
Chichester.

George Fossick

The artist George Fossick produced a number of fine line drawings of local scenes between the wars. This is his depiction of the war memorial in Eastgate Square.

The war memorial with St Pancras's Church in the background. In about 1940 the memorial was moved to a quieter site in a nearby park because Eastgate Square was becoming too noisy a thoroughfare in which to hold services of remembrance!

Eastgate Square, 1972. The brick buildings which dominate this picture now accommodate rather smarter shops and restaurants. Note the old cinema in the background with its 'Granada' lettering. This was formerly the Corn Exchange, built by George Draper, a local architect, in 1833. By the end of the nineteenth century it was also used for social and theatrical events, and films began to be shown there in 1910. It is now a McDonald's restaurant.

This undistinguished town house in the Hornet in the 1960s is just a stone's throw from Chichester's Georgian gracefulness. In the 1990s the Hornet has become an intriguing mixture of new development and traditional family businesses on the fringes of the city centre.

This thatched barn looks rural enough but in fact stands on the corner of the Hornet and Needlemakers. At the time the picture was taken (August 1972), it was owned by Combes Garden Centre; it has since become the garden centre's main shopping complex.

The Nag's Head (or Nags) in St Pancras is one of Chichester's best known pubs. This picture shows the inn sign and its artist, Bill Welcome.

The fifteenth-century splendour of the Cathedral bell-tower overlooks Tower Street, complete with Ford Anglia, in this 1960s picture. It is the only detached cathedral bell-tower in England. It is also known as Raymonds or Rymonds Tower after a fourteenth-century lord of the manor of Apuldram. He bought stone to fortify his manor but was forbidden to do so by Edward III and the stone was sold or given to Bishop Langton who started building the Bell Tower.

This photograph shows a splendid combination of nature's tranquillity and man's craftsmanship. The cattle are grazing in Westgate fields; indeed they used to graze right up to the city walls. The busy Avenue de Chartres has destroyed this idyllic scene.

This famous view of the Cathedral was taken during the rebuilding work which followed the collapse of the spire on 21 February 1861. Prior to its collapse the tower and spire had already been deemed structurally unsound. Massive timbers had been shoring up the building while repair work continued. During a violent storm on the fateful day the stonework began to disintegrate and the workmen were evacuated. Ninety minutes later, some 6,000 tons of masonry fell straight into the Cathedral. Incredibly nobody was injured. Work on the new spire began in 1865, and it was capped by a weathervane on 28 June 1866. A perfect replica of the original spire, it was designed by Sir Gilbert Scott and built at a cost of £53,000.

An aerial photograph of Chichester, looking north-east, taken by Aerofilms, *c*. 1960 (the postmark on the reverse is dated 1963). With the growth of air travel after the Second World War, aerial photography became increasingly popular. This photograph demonstrates the dominance of the Cathedral not only over the city but also over the magnificent countryside which surrounds it. The Summersdale housing development, which was to obliterate the attractive countryside shown in the top left-hand corner of this picture, has yet to be built.

Many of Chichester's streets and squares are named after former Cathedral clergy. Hannah Square in the Parklands Estate is named after this man, the Very Reverend John Julius Hannah, who was dean of Chichester between 1912 and 1927.

FUNERAL OF THE LATE
BISHOP OF CHICHESTER
(DR. WILBERFORCE)
Nº 6
P.P.Co.   SEP. 14th 1907.

This impressive array of lay vicars (Cathedral choir members) and Cathedral clergy is processing along Canon Lane on the occasion of the funeral of Dr Wilberforce.

Believed to be the only photograph in this book which was taken from a balloon, this picture provides an excellent overview of the city looking east towards Tangmere and Oving in the 1960s.

Throughout this century, Chichester Cathedral has been a focal point for visitors. This postcard depicts some of the fine Saxon sculptures which have been admired by tourists for many years. The Cathedral was built on the site of the Saxon church of St Peter. Building began during the episcopate of Bishop Ralph Luffa between 1091 and 1123. The eastern end of the Cathedral was dedicated in 1123 but major building work continued during the next two centuries. Bishop Luffa is still remembered, for his name has been given to Chichester's principal mixed comprehensive school.

The cathedral spire can just be seen poking out above the buildings on the south side of East Street in this late nineteenth-century view.

The photographer of this postcard view did a splendid job, showing both the Cross and the Cathedral spire from East Street. The postcard was published by Raphael Tuck & Sons who described themselves as 'Fine Art Publishers to Their Majesties The King and Queen and to Her Majesty Queen Mary'.

Chichester Barracks, *c.* 1905. The main Chichester to Midhurst thoroughfare (now the A286) runs beside it.

Bishop Otter College is now part of the West Sussex Institute of Higher Education. Its most distinctive feature is its modern chapel, shown here under construction in the mid-1960s.

Shippams's factory, 1952. Founded in Chichester in 1750, Shippams became world famous for their meat and fish pastes. They even supplied foods for Captain Scott's ill-fated expedition to the South Pole in 1903.

Lunchtime at Acford's printers, *c.* 1950. The company was based in Terminus Road in the south-west of the city but has now ceased trading. The man at the back on the left is Hector Amey.

The interior of Prior's wool factory. The street known as Woolstaplers is the only surviving reminder of Ebenezer Prior's wool factory which stood on Tower Street. The man on the left is Will Langley.

The baling area in Prior's wool factory. The mustachioed man on the left is George Langley, Will's father (see page 29).

Wool-sorting in Prior's wool factory. Like Acford's, Prior's has long since ceased to exist, and Tower Street is now dominated by the splendid library with the county council offices immediately behind.

Lord Edmund Talbot was an MP in the Chichester area before the First World War; this picture depicts a 'complimentary dinner' held in his honour on 25 April 1913. It is an almost exclusively male company, with a remarkable number of moustaches! Lord Talbot's brother was the Duke of Norfolk until his death in the 1890s.

(B)

RSH & SON
CHESTER

H.M. THE KING INSPECTS THE
W.S. NATIONAL RESERVES
AT CHICHESTER JULY 28/13

King George V inspects the National Reserves in Chichester in July 1919. This was not the king's only visit to Chichester (see page 35). Note the splendid beard of the man standing sixth from the left in the front row.

Known as Truffle Cottage, this house in St Paul's Road once served as a toll house on the north-western approach to the city. The thatch later caught fire and was replaced by tiles. The building is still recognizable today (105 St Paul's Road) and can be found between the junctions with Parklands Road and Sherborne Road.

One of Chichester's oldest buildings, St Mary's Hospital dates from the end of the thirteenth century. It formerly provided temporary accommodation for travellers and the sick, as well as 'aged people of good life and religion'; it has now been split into almshouses offering accommodation for four married couples and eight single persons.

Miss Reagan and Miss Pearce, two aged inmates of St Mary's Hospital who were interviewed by King Edward VII. Edward VII reigned from 1901 until 1910.

Chichester Infirmary was built between 1825 and 1828 by George Draper, although there have been numerous additions. It became the Royal West Sussex Hospital in 1913 on the occasion of the visit of George V, shown above. The wisteria shown on the hospital walls is believed to be the oldest in the country and originated in China. The lower picture is another example of George Fossick's work. Patients moved out of the hospital building in 1973 and the premises were then used to house regional hospital management and administration staff. In 1982 it became the headquarters of Chichester Health Authority. Meanwhile, patients were housed in huts in the grounds – the last of them moved out of the huts in June 1990. The health authority vacated the premises in March 1995 and work is under way to convert the building into a prestigious block of flats.

Royal West Sussex Hospital.   George Fossick

Graylingwell Hospital, to the north of Chichester, accommodated a number of soldiers wounded in Flanders in the First World War. Judging by the empty beds and smart poses, things were not unduly hectic when these pictures were taken. Graylingwell has since become the Chichester area's principal mental hospital, but as the century draws to a close its future hangs in the balance.

The Pirate King and Ruth ganging up on Frederic in the Chichester Amateur Operatic Society's production of *The Pirates of Penzance* in 1925. This was also the first show ever to be staged by the Society in January 1911. The Society had been founded in 1910 by a group of Cicestrians – lay vicars from the Cathedral and local businessmen and their wives – who were keen to produce for themselves the relatively new and very popular operas of Gilbert & Sullivan. They performed exclusively Gilbert & Sullivan operas until 1930. The first secretary of the Society was Reginald Stewart, a lay vicar at the Cathedral and later ordained priest. He played the Pirate King in the first production of *The Pirates of Penzance* in 1911. Numerous more secular businesses were represented in the Society in its formative years including L. Chaffer from Chaffer's Printers; Miss Charge from the drapers at the Cross; Mr and Mrs Dawtrey, electricians; Humphry, tobacconists; Kimbell, pork butchers; and Purchase, coal merchants. Until 1976 the Society performed predominantly Gilbert & Sullivan shows. This was largely because the Society's long-standing producer, Margo Pink (who joined in 1919), had a passion for the works of Gilbert & Sullivan. After her death in 1976, the Society's repertoire widened significantly into pantomimes, music hall and modern musicals such as *Carousel* and *Oklahoma!* Until the Second World War, the Society performed at the Corn Exchange. After the war they moved to the Assembly Room in North Street, where they have performed ever since. Performances are also given in the Minerva Studio Theatre.

The Pirate King from the Society's 1925 production. Although only three performances of *The Pirates of Penzance* were given in January 1911, shows soon ran for a whole week. Matinée performances were both the most popular and the most expensive.

'Dramatic pose' seems something of an understatement in describing this picture of Mad Margaret from the Society's 1926 offering, *Ruddigore*.

The year 1928 saw the Society tackle *HMS Pinafore*. In this picture Dick Deadeye does his wonderful best to spoil the otherwise immaculate group! The man just left of centre, playing Sir Joseph Porter, was W.T. ('Will') Cole who ran Slindon post office and who played all the Gilbert & Sullivan patter song parts until the early 1950s. He had played Major-General Stanley in the Society's first ever performance of *The Pirates of Penzance* in 1911.

The curtain call for the Society's concert performance of *Jolly Roger* in March 1936. The Society has always had a reputation for strong choral singing. The lady in the centre of the front row, just to the left of the skull and crossbones, is Joyce Foote, who was the Society's pianist. This was one of the Society's early departures from the work of Gilbert & Sullivan; the earliest were *Dorothy* in 1930 and *Merrie England* in 1931.

One of the Society's more ambitious ventures was *Merrie England* under canvas. In 1952 they gave a number of open air performances of this opera in Priory Park, against a splendid backcloth of Windsor Castle. There was a cast of over one hundred, with chorus members picked from local societies, and guest soloists including Anne Ziegler, Webster Booth and Leslie Rands. The latter was a soloist with the D'Oyly Carte Opera Company but his roots were in Chichester; he was the son of a Chichester hairdresser, who practised in East Street. Mr Rand senior and his wife were founder members of the Society. Crowds came in large numbers to see the show, and a goodly sum was raised for an eventide housing project on the outskirts of the city.

'Schoolgirls we eighteen and under. . . .' A colourfully dressed girls' chorus and bright backcloth helps to lift the gloom of postwar austerity in this production of *The Mikado* by the Society in 1950.

One of the more dramatic scenes in the Society's 1955 production of *Ruddigore*, the moment when the ghosts appear from their picture frames.

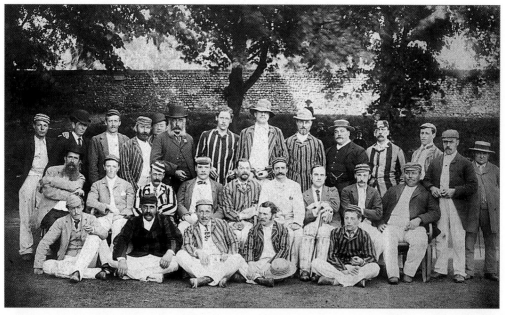

The Priory Park cricket team towards the end of the nineteenth century. Cricket was first played in Priory Park in 1851. The team's most famous player was James Lillywhite, who captained the first England side to play against Australia in 1877. Priory Park, on the site of a Franciscan friary which was dissolved in 1538, has become an immensely popular area not just for cricket but also for concerts, shows and firework displays.

Chichester railway station at the turn of the century. This view is frequently published and is the one most people associate with the city. But we should not forget Chichester's other railway station: hidden behind the station buildings, towards the top left of the picture, is the Chichester terminus of the Selsey Tramway which opened only a few years before this picture was taken. The building on the right has for many years been the Globe public house. The area immediately to the right of the station buildings has been transformed, with a new Waitrose supermarket appearing in 1992 and proposals for the construction of a nightclub close by just a few years later.

An early picture of the Chichester Festival Theatre which opened in 1962 and today is one of southern England's leading theatres. The area of green in the foreground is now occupied by the Minerva Studio Theatre which opened in 1988.

Three 1980s picture postcard views of Chichester. Acre's, next to Marks & Spencer, has since closed; it is just one of many businesses that have shut in the city centre during the late 1980s and 1990s.

One of the most traumatic events in Chichester's recent history was the Great Storm on 16 October 1987. These scenes of devastation were photographed in the Summersdale area after the storm.

Until recently the Royal Military Police March was a regular feature of Chichester's year, involving thousands of soldiers and civilians. The march traditionally culminated in a parade through the streets of Chichester. Here an assortment of weary walkers make their way down North Street in 1989.

Sainsbury's Superstore at Chichester was destroyed by fire on 16 December 1993, an event which made the national news. This picture shows the shell of the burnt-out building. In the foreground the A27 is submerged in the floodwater that again elevated Chichester to the national headlines just three weeks later.

WEST OF CHICHESTER

My clockwise tour of the villages within a 5-mile radius of Chichester begins to the west of the city and includes the large villages of Fishbourne and Bosham as well as the smaller communities of West Ashling, East Ashling and Funtington. Bosham has become well known as a tourist centre and understandably there has never been a shortage of photographers wishing to capture its unique surroundings on film. Thanks to the magnificent efforts of Angela Bromley-Martin, Bosham has a superb photographic record; for this reason it dominates this section. As with Chichester itself, I have attempted to reflect the community aspects of the villages as well as their tourist aspects. With the exception of the Roman Palace at Fishbourne, there has been little to draw photographers to the other villages, and pictures of them are consequently more elusive. The material that is available, however, demonstrates that economic change has affected them as much as Chichester; the modern traveller through Fishbourne or West Ashling will see no evidence of Boys' Garage or Heather's Stores. The present-day West Ashling resident will have to travel further in search of his sausages!

Boys' Garage, *c.* 1932. The garage was a well-known feature of the main street in Fishbourne. It was built in 1927 and demolished in the mid-1980s when the new A27 was built.

Houses at Creek End Corner, near Boys' Garage on the main road through Fishbourne, 1946. These cottages were originally constructed between 1825 and 1830 as artisans' dwellings. During the Second World War they fell into neglect and were boarded up. Later they were refurbished by an architect named Reynish. The first owners of the newly refurbished house were Mr George Bevis (of Eastgate Pharmacy) and his wife.

Growing fresh fruit and vegetables always has been – and still is – an important aspect of Sussex country life, as shown by these greenhouses between Fishbourne and Bosham, captured on film in the 1930s. The Downs form a splendid backcloth in the top picture. Since these photographs were taken, the coastal plain between Chichester and Portsmouth has become increasingly urbanized.

The Church of St Peter and St Mary, Fishbourne. The church was described by Ian Nairn and Nikolaus Pevsner as 'attractive at first glance, but in fact almost all indifferent nineteenth century'! Rebuilding took place in 1821 and again in 1847 when the nave was added. The lower picture suggests an air of isolation and remoteness which the church no longer enjoys; it is now separated from the vicarage by the A27 dual carriageway and road noise has caused problems which were unimaginable at the time this picture was taken!

A swan poses for the camera at Millpond Cottage, West Ashling. The mill sluice still controls the level of the mill-pond. The adjacent watermill was operational until 1939. In the summer of 1976 the mill-pond dried up in the drought and great cracks appeared at the bottom.

Shortly before alteration work began, this is the Richmond Arms at West Ashling, c. 1905. Lambert & Norris signs can still be seen today; one example is outside the Bush in the Hornet, Chichester.

The Richmond Arms after modernization, *c.* 1915. What a lot of changes have taken place! It is still possible to identify Millpond Cottage immediately behind it. The pub is still going strong eighty years later.

The mill-pond and mill at West Ashling. The basic brick structure, latterly known as Hacketts Mill, was built in 1825 as a watermill for corn milling, but between 1832 and 1850 it was used for making paper pulp from rags, one of only six such mills in the whole of Sussex. Subsequently flour was milled here until production stopped in the 1930s. Armfields, Hampshire millwrights who specialized in improving traditional watermills, erected the windmill on piers built up inside the mill between 1859 and 1861. A turbine was later fitted instead of a water wheel. The sweeps were removed in 1922 when an ailing inhabitant of the village found the noise disturbing! Mr Hackett is seen here on the pond shortly before the sweeps were removed.

The view westwards along the street in West Ashling, *c.* 1930. The sails of the windmill can just be seen in the background. The shop on the left is Heather's General Store, noted for home-baked bread and home-made pork sausages.

East Ashling is a pleasant though unremarkable village on the Chichester–Funtington road. Its most distinguished building is the partially Elizabethan Ashling House. Originally East Ashling Grange was quaintly named Cucumber Cottage.

Pupils at Funtington School in the 1920s. The inscription on the slate at the front confirms the class number. The school dates from 1873 when a National School for children up to the age of fourteen was erected on village common land. National Schools were church schools that were set up under the auspices of the National Society for the Education of the Poor in the Principles of the Established Church.

Two contrasting modes of travel meet in the main street at Funtington in the 1950s; a cyclist on a penny farthing rides past a garage with the distinctive BP logo.

The Fox & Hounds, Funtington, *c.* 1905. The inn is thought to be three hundred years old. In 1958 it was described as 'an inn of character, cosy and comfortable . . . where the locals are always ready to accept a challenge of darts or shove-halfpenny'.

Wheels aplenty, on prams and bicycle, decorate Bosham High Street in this more recent view.

Humphrey Selwyn Lloyd took this picture of Bosham Church and Quay Meadow in 1903. He lived in the Bosham Manor House for many years and was an enthusiastic photographer.

Bosham Church looms over the blacksmith's cottage at the Apse shipyard, Quay Meadow. From here were launched vessels of up to 500 tons, the last being *The Good Hoper* launched in July 1903.

Pauline Collins, daughter of Bosham's postmaster, pictured outside her father's shop. Pauline delivered mail and telegrams for her father. Although she is shown here in the first quarter of the century, her attire would hardly look out of place in the 1990s.

Everything from Weetabix to du Maurier tobacco seems to be available at Bosham Country Stores, situated a few doors down from the Congregational Church (now the United Reformed Church) in Bosham Lane. In 1899 the premises had become a money order, telegram and telegraphic office managed by Harry Collins, the sub-postmaster, who in 1907 also opened a shop on the premises. At the back of the shop he had the first telephone exchange in Bosham. On his death in 1922 his son took over as sub-postmaster. In 1947 the post office moved to the High Street and the Coward family then ran the shop as the Country Stores for many years.

The proprietors Mr and Mrs Colbourne and the staff pose outside Ye Olde Bosham Tea Shoppe in Bosham Lane. Records show that George Perver was the baker here in 1862. In 1891 Ernest Layzell helped his mother-in-law, George's widow, to run the bakery but it was not successful. Two deliveries of bread were made daily when this picture was taken in about 1910. The building is now a private house called Loafers.

The Swiss village fête in Vicarage Gardens, Bosham, 6/7 July 1904. The vicarage is now Walton House and Oakcroft Nurseries occupy the former gardens.

BOSHAM WAR MEMORIAL UNVEILED ARMISTICE DAY. SUNDAY NOV 11. 192

The unveiling of Bosham war memorial on Armistice Day, 11 November 1923. The ceremony was carried out by the Revd J.W. Maunder, vicar of Bosham. It was built entirely by voluntary labour; the builders were Collis Chapman, Bob Brierly, Harry Grender, George Ede, Tom Newell and Jim Ede.

Harry Apps and C. Snellgrove are two of the boys sitting on the steps of Quay Cottage, Bosham, beside the mill.

The Anchor pub in the High Street, Bosham, *c.* 1900. Ale has probably been sold here for several centuries, and there is reputed to be an underground tunnel which runs to the church. Two doors down was another pub, the Ship. At one time the two pubs are run by the Martin brothers in competition with each other. The thatched buildings opposite the Anchor are thought to have been pigsties. The Ship served as an officers' club during the Second World War and the artist Rex Whistler (1905–44) painted murals of some of the local characters on the walls.

Fishermen mending their nets alongside the mill at Bosham. The mill has since been rebuilt by Lord Iveagh for the Bosham Sailing Club, using as much of the original material, such as bricks and tiles, as possible.

This granite barge was probably owned by A.H. Edwards, coal, coke, wood, oil, gravel, grit and sand merchants. Bosham service station now stands on the site of their yard.

Spectators on board the *Excel* at a Bosham regatta in either 1910 or 1912. The man standing by the mast is probably Harry Martin, who owned the ship. Note the wide range of headgear – hats were evidently popular as only one of the spectators seems to be without one.

A ship at Bosham Quay in the late 1940s. It is believed to have been carrying shingle and gravel to repair Bosham Quay.

The Manor House party watching the Bosham regatta in 1901 or 1902. This photograph is attributable to Humphrey Selwyn Lloyd, owner of the Manor House.

Bosham has always been a magnet for visitors but it has also been a busy workaday place. Here Bill and Jack Arnold are loading their nets alongside the Quay.

The tidal waters at Bosham provide a constantly changing vista for the photographer. Here a schooner is seen alongside the Quay at low tide with a fisherman mending nets in the foreground.

Quay Meadow at Bosham has always been a paradise for strollers, although present day visitors must leave their cars elsewhere. In the early 1920s, however, people could park on the quay. Chidham can be seen just over the water.

This large crowd is enjoying the greasy pole competition, which was a popular sideshow at the 1913 regatta on Bosham Quay. The first prize in this competition was a leg of mutton. Note the fashion in swimwear!

Many motorists have had cause to regret leaving their cars by the water at Bosham at low tide. This is a particularly strong high tide at Street End in about 1937. The house on the left used to be the town hall before the move to Westbourne. The house was converted into three cottages but has now reverted to being one house.

NORTH OF CHICHESTER

This section focuses on Lavant, the principal village to the north of Chichester. Lavant is actually three villages, each with its own identity: West Lavant is the most modest community and its existence is barely acknowledged on maps of the area, Mid Lavant is the sprawling village on the busy A286, and East Lavant is the pretty village by the river in the valley. The three civil parishes combined in 1872 and the ecclesiastical parishes combined in 1880.

Mid Lavant used to have a railway, and while this is now defunct the road gets busier every year. What, however, can one say of a river which in some years never appears and yet in other years appears with such force that whole communities are placed under siege?

I am especially grateful to Mary Ninness whose splendid collection of photographs ensured that the following selection includes more recent highlights of Lavant life.

Mid Lavant, *c.* 1910. On the left is the post office. When it closed in 1972 a new post office opened at Lavant Down.

Although Nikolaus Pevsner and Ian Nairn described Mid Lavant as 'spoilt by heavy traffic and oddly straggling and boring', this picture shows a more picturesque area of the village. This is the view across the Lavant valley from the main road, photographed in the 1950s; the scene has changed little over the last fifty years.

The centre of Mid Lavant in the 1950s. The single white line in the centre of the road has now vanished completely. Compare this with the photograph opposite, taken nearly fifty years before.

The Lavant Home, a classic Sussex flint and brick house, was a girls' orphanage at the time this picture was taken, *c.* 1900. The building is shown on at least three maps of the area between 1873 and 1914.

A thatched house with a crooked chimney in East Lavant, early 1900s. The name Lavant means 'landspring' – a reminder of the stream which occasionally flows through the village.

Major Low's funeral, 1921. Major Low lived in Lavant House and died after a heart attack while on his way to London to change his will for the benefit of his extended family! Lavant House later became a school.

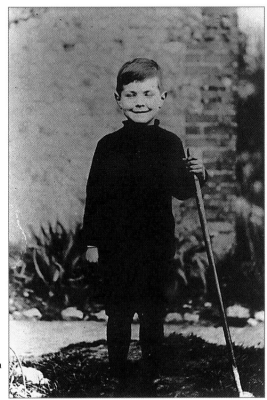

'Smile, please!' This is Bert Foster at the tender age of three. Born in 1896, he lived in Sheepwash Lane, East Lavant, and became a butcher in Chichester.

The River Lavant has always been most capricious, appearing only after periods of heavy winter rainfall. The ducks here are certainly fortunate!

Sheep used to be dipped in the river by Wyatt's Yard in Lavant and penned on the corner of the village green where the war memorial is today. The thatched sheds accommodated Mr Foster's blacksmith's forge; it is hardly surprising that horseshoes were found during excavations of the river silt in November 1975.

It is hard to believe that this gentle stream, pictured at East Lavant nearly a century ago, could be anything but tranquil. But in 1960 and again in 1994 it burst its banks and flooded the surrounding countryside, causing chaos!

The 1970 Lavant Festival was a hugely popular village event; MP Christopher Chataway arrived at the festival aboard the old fire engine.

Another photograph from the Lavant Festival, 1970. An intriguing game is in progress on the village green. In the car is Maurice Shears, his efforts watched by Mr Lovegrove. In his book *Sussex Villages*, Michael Baker related that a complaint was once received about youngsters playing golf on the village green; it was alleged that this 'interfered with the comfort of other users of the green, cut up the turf and resulted in balls very nearly smashing through windows'. An irate parent retorted that the green was the only safe place for village boys to play and that no action should be taken provided that no annoyance was caused and the divots were trodden back in!

Accidents will happen. This Haslemere bus fell foul of the icy conditions at Burchers Corner, Mid Lavant, in the late 1920s.

Despite the casualties of the First World War, Lavant Football Club continued to thrive in the postwar years. This team photograph from the 1919/20 season includes A. Sawtell, G. Ware, H. Bussell, C. Lock, S. Squires, E. Hayler, H. Lock, W. Millier, R. Penfold and D. Pearce. During this season the team finished runners-up in the Midhurst & District League.

A proud moment: Kim Hinkley of Lavant receives her Queen's Guide Award in the late 1970s. Among the other Guides in the picture are Sue Tester, Rosalind Cummins, Julie Hellyer, Nicola Jupp and Clare Howlett.

Lavant House was originally built as a dower house for the dukes of Richmond and Gordon. It became a school in 1952. Dora Green, the school's co-founder, recalled: 'We ended 1952 with ten names on the register; we started 1953 with twenty. It was like a child who continually grows out of her dresses before her mother can catch up.'

Pupils of the very last class at West Stoke School, pictured outside the present village hall in 1921.

Pupils of Lavant School, 1924. Mr A.J. Woodman was the school's headmaster at the turn of the century; his son S. Woodman ran Woodman's Stores which stocked a goodly selection of sweets, tobacco and cigarettes. One wonders how many pupils were castigated by Woodman senior for eating sweets in class bought from Woodman junior! Note the rather cumbersome footwear of those sitting in the front row — it is interesting to reflect that boots like these have become fashionable in the 1990s!

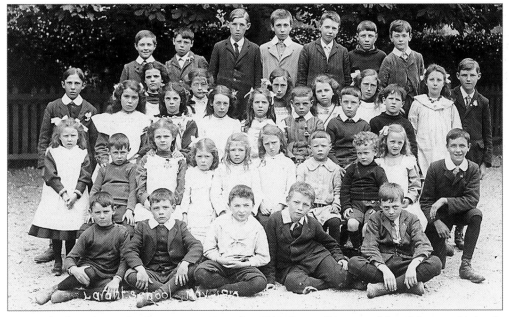

Lavant School pupils pose for the camera in November 1915. Presumably most of their fathers would already have gone — or were about to go — to war; conscription was introduced just two months later. Mr Woodman, the headmaster, died in rather less auspicious circumstances; he fell off his bicycle and fractured his skull.

During the drought years of 1989 and 1990, nobody could have believed that the little River Lavant would ever come to life again. However, in January 1994 the river, which had failed to flow at all in three of the five previous years, became a torrent, burst its banks and submerged the roads and much of the village green at East Lavant. The area round the village hall was particularly badly affected.

This is one of a splendid collection of photographs taken in 1985 to mark the opening of the newly extended Lavant School in Mid Lavant. By then, of course, there were two schools in Lavant, the girls' private school Lavant House having opened over thirty years before. Mary Ninness, who kindly provided all these pictures of Lavant School, informs me that before the new building in 1985 there were two separate school buildings, one in East Lavant and one in Mid Lavant, and pupils had to march from one school to the other for lunch. These uniformed pupils certainly look rather smarter than their 1924 and 1915 counterparts!

This is the first of a sequence of six previously unpublished photographs of farming life in the heavily farmed land north-west of Lavant (towards Chilgrove) taken in August 1932. More than any other photographs in this book they capture the spirit of past times and I am immensely grateful to John Herniman for his permission to reproduce them. Here, hay is being picked up with a wheel-driven loader.

A traction engine used for threshing. A flat belt from the large flywheel on the far side of the engine drove the threshing machine, either outdoors or in the centre of a barn, both ends of which were filled with sheaves. Once the sheaves had been threshed, the straw was thrown out through the doors on the far side of the barn and stacked in the yard. The grain was sacked off at the rear end of the threshing machine and carried away.

Threshing outdoors, August 1932.

Work begins on yet another haystack; the elevator is not yet required.

Bill Short cutting wheat with a reaper-binder.

Ploughing with a hired Fordson tractor, a two-furrow plough and furrow press.

These two photographs show the Chichester–Midhurst railway line which opened in 1881 with stations at Lavant, Singleton and Cocking. Although passenger services were withdrawn in 1935, freight services to Cocking and Singleton persisted until closure of both stations on 28 August 1953. Lavant station remained open and in 1954 the north end of the platform was surfaced in concrete to facilitate the loading of sugar beet. Between 1963 and 1970, when the station closed completely, it was a central loading point for sugar beet. In 1972 gravel extraction started nearby, and a condition of the planning consent was that the gravel should be removed by rail from a point just south of Lavant station. Gravel extraction ceased in the early 1990s.

Lavant was the first stop on the Chichester–Midhurst line. Like the other station buildings on the line, it was designed by J.L. Myers. The mock Tudor timber-framing was a hallmark of Myers' work. Later on the Lavant station building had to be partially tile-hung to address the problem of damp. The railway line itself is now a cycle track known as Centurion Way, although many environmentalists believe the track should be relaid for trains in order to provide an alternative to road transport.

Lavant station was rather a sad sight by 1971. Although passenger services had been withdrawn many years before, the station was used as a central loading point for sugar beet and remained open until 1970. Note the graffiti on the side wall. Twenty-five years on, the station building has become part of a smart housing development.

EAST OF CHICHESTER

Three villages are predominant in this section, two of which have been well served by photographers because of their particular – and very contrasting – attractions. Boxgrove, although a vibrant community in its own right, also offers a fragment of priceless English heritage – its priory church and priory ruins. Tangmere is rather different; its now defunct fighter air base served a vital role in defending Britain from invasion during the Second World War. Some of the images of Tangmere give us a glimpse of a frightening period in Britain's history, and contrast with the pictures of Boxgrove Priory with its sense of permanence and serenity.

   The third village, Halnaker, is best known for its mill, immortalized by Sussex writer Hilaire Belloc; however, I have concentrated on the changing heart of the village and in particular the development of Stane Street from a peaceful thoroughfare at the turn of the century to a busy motor road sixty years later.

Although it is now sadly no more, Tangmere Aerodrome enjoyed a long and distinguished history. It was established in 1917 and came into use in March 1918. In 1939 it became Sector Headquarters in No. 11 Group, Fighter Command, and proved to be a vital front-line airfield, especially during the Battle of Britain. Its strategic importance was not lost on the Germans; on 16 August 1940, a brilliant sunny day, a large force of Junkers dive-bombers mounted a devastating attack on the airfield, leaving many personnel dead and injured. But the base rallied and during the warm sunny days of early September the fighters from Tangmere were in constant action. As Bob Ogley recalled: 'The Germans returned to their bases leaving a parched Sussex countryside littered with the smoking wrecks of [their] aircraft.' As the threat of invasion receded, Tangmere-based crews provided bomber escorts and flew patrols over France. By September 1944 Tangmere's fighters had destroyed 866 enemy aircraft and damaged a further 440. The base was disbanded in June 1958.

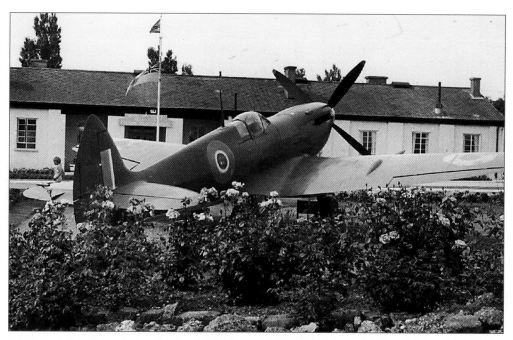

A Spitfire at Tangmere. During the Battle of Britain, squadrons from the Tangmere section were in the air on each day that bombing raids were attempted in southern England.

Tangmere hosted many 'mobile wings' practising manoeuvring between airfields in readiness for the advance after the invasion of Europe. These two Canadian pilots of 127 Wing are pictured at Tangmere in May 1944.

Lysander pick-up pilots from 161 Squadron at Tangmere in 1943. Left to right: Flt-Lt R. Hooper, Flg Off. J. McCairns, Flt-Lt P. Vaughan Fowler, Sqn Ldr H. Verity, Flg Off. B. Rymills (with Henry the dog), Flt-Lt S. Hankey.

An RE8 at Tangmere in 1918. Note the hangars under construction in the background.

Arguably the highlight of Tangmere's life was the visit of King George VI on 14 July 1944. He came to present honours to RAF personnel on the base, reflecting the important role Tangmere had played during the D-Day landings.

St Andrew's Church, Tangmere. It is described by Ian Nairn and Nikolaus Pevsner as a 'very simple, decent building'. The nave dates back to the twelfth century and the spire is thought to date from the thirteenth century.

Before the RAF arrived, Tangmere was an unremarkable village, probably of Saxon origin. A manor at Tangmere is mentioned in the Domesday Book. It seems that for many centuries the population of the village remained at around 100 or 150, reaching a peak of 225 in 1841. This wonderful picture of the village postboy in Church Lane, taken in about 1895, reflects its tranquil nature. In his book *Sussex Villages*, Michael Baker relates that outside the church porch stands an ancient yew tree with a hollow trunk so large that it has been used to store the churchyard roller!

The heart of Tangmere, *c.* 1935. This picture illustrates Tangmere's peaceful past. Sadly the pond has now gone, the population is approaching 3,000 and the road to the right is now often congested with users of the 'One Stop' village store.

To the north is Halnaker, which has suffered no such population explosion. This postcard of Halnaker and its beautifully dressed youngsters dates from 1910, and bears a Halnaker postmark. The postmaster at the time is thought to have been Fred Gardner.

The present Halnaker House is the work of architect Sir Edwin Lutyens and was built in 1938 in neo-Georgian style. Ian Nairn and Nikolaus Pevsner described it as 'late and sober, almost dowdy'.

Both these pictures show exactly the same view – the village store at Halnaker. The top picture was taken in 1910, when the store was owned by Mr Pennicott; in the lower picture, the owner was Mr Wheatley. Curiously, on the lower picture the location has erroneously been described as Boxgrove.

Cattle on this busy thoroughfare between Chichester and Guildford would be a most unusual and alarming sight nowadays. This photograph depicts the last time that cows were brought through Halnaker village, in the early 1960s. The cows were owned by Harry Parker, the former landlord of the Anglesey Arms.

Halnaker's main street. The post office, just visible on the right, was demolished in the early 1950s.

Tom McCarthy poses for the camera outside Hat Hill Cottage near Halnaker, a splendid example of a Sussex flint-and-brick building. Tom was a gamekeeper on the Goodwood Estate for some sixty-five years.

This woman strolls nonchalantly with her child along the road in Halnaker in 1907. They are walking on Stane Street – the Roman road built to link London and Chichester – which runs straight through Halnaker.

This is the view up Stane Street in Halnaker, showing the sturdy flint-and-brick buildings and garden walls of Adelaide Cottages. Villagers used to draw water from the well outside the cottages. Note the absence of traffic, reflecting the village's tranquillity.

Stane Street in Halnaker in the early 1960s. Motor transport has arrived: note the speed limit sign and the pavement to protect pedestrians from the perils of motor transport.

The ruins of the former Halnaker House will doubtless be readily recognized by travellers approaching Halnaker from Chichester. Built in medieval times by the de Haye family (who also founded Boxgrove Priory), the house was completely remodelled in the sixteenth century; sadly it had become derelict by about 1800.

Football enthusiasts will probably think of Norwich City FC when 'The Canaries' are mentioned; fewer people know that this is also the nickname of Boxgrove Football Club, pictured here in about 1912. The colours of their strip were red and yellow.

Children playing what appears to be a game of marbles in the main street of Boxgrove, *c*. 1910. The entrance to Church Lane is just visible in the foreground on the right.

This is the view looking north along Boxgrove's main street, *c*. 1930. Although dominated by the priory, Boxgrove has always been a busy community in its own right. In his book *Sussex Garland*, Tony Wales recalls the Boxgrove Tipteers who in 1920 revived the tradition of mumming, a type of informal Christmas entertainment, with carols and folksongs including 'The Moon Shone Bright' and 'Sweet Rosy Morn', as well as a 'dance over the sticks'.

Boxgrove's main street, between the wars. In the Domesday Book Boxgrove is mentioned as 'Bosgrove', but one early writer thought Boxgrove was named after a green tree, which he considered highly appropriate because it 'grows and flourishes with virtues'.

This is the view from further south along Boxgrove's main street. Many visitors to its famous priory church come this way. A.S. Cooke, in *Off the Beaten Track*, addresses such visitors thus: 'As you approach it, a sense of the medieval gradually possesses your mind. In these material days it may be rash to attribute this impression to that invisible aura or emanation which may proceed from such sacred or venerable walls . . . but the feeling is there.'

Visitors coming to Boxgrove Priory from the north cannot miss this splendid building, Priory Cottage, which stands by the approach road. The middle part of the house dates back 200 years and in recent times it has been used as a restaurant and also as a butcher's shop!

This postcard shows the former vicarage at Boxgrove, its stonework masked by ivy, *c.* 1900. The vicarage used to be where Priory Gate House now stands and was demolished in the late 1930s. Presumably the man struggling to control the dogs is the vicar himself!

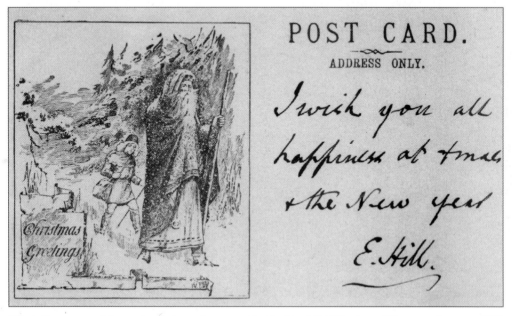

This is the reverse of the postcard above. It was sent by the Revd E. Hill, vicar of Boxgrove between 1891 and 1911. Note how the X in 'Xmas' has been drawn at an angle, more like a cross – perhaps the vicar was trying to put Christ back into Christmas!

The view looking south along Boxgrove's main street, 1950s. The shop on the right is still doing good business forty years later.

The view south along the upper part of Boxgrove's main street, *c.* 1932. Visitors coming to the priory from London would follow this road. As Cooke nostalgically pointed out, 'One wishes that the enthusiasm which inspired our forefathers to tramp long miles over dangerous roads to kneel before the shrines of St Mary and St Blaise in Boxgrove Church could still inspire all Sussex folk in these degenerate days to do likewise.'

Priory Farm, adjoining the priory ruins at Boxgrove, photographed in the 1930s. The farmhouse is now a smart private dwelling and offices have recently been added.

The priory and its church are undoubtedly the most important features of Boxgrove. The priory was a daughter house of the Abbey of Lessay in Normandy, France. This is the remains of the splendid stonework in the lower part of the north wall of the old church.

Boxgrove Priory dates from Norman times. In 1108 Robert de Haye, who had become Lord of Halnaker, donated land at **Boxgrove** to the Abbey at Lessay. The Abbot immediately sent three of his monks to oversee the construction of the priory and take possession. This picture shows the ivy-covered remains of the Norman chapter house, photographed in the late 1940s. The ivy has since been trimmed back significantly!

Boxgrove Priory Church from the south, 1920s. Note the rather clumsy etching of the caption (as with the lower picture on page 105)! Cooke is convinced of the spiritual benefit of a visit to the church: 'then would the sight of noble arch and column, chantry tomb and mullioned window bring exaltation to the spirit'.

Boxgrove Priory Church and ruins, photographed from the north in the late 1940s. This view remains almost unchanged to the present day.

George Fossick's depiction of the interior of Boxgrove Priory Church scarcely does justice to its magnificence. The nave is a wonderful example of early English architecture, dating from about 1220.

George Fossick's work, completed between the wars, was prepared as postcards for Moore (spelt Moor on some postcards) & Wingham, the forerunners of Moore & Tillyer. Their stationery shop in East Street, Chichester, closed as recently as 1996 but their printing business is still going strong in the city.

The priory church at Boxgrove is often mistakenly referred to as the priory but the caption on this splendid photograph, taken from the north-east, has it right. Cattle used to be a common sight on priory land. In 1622 six parishioners were prosecuted for playing cricket in the churchyard.

These are the ruins of a fine three-storeyed building built in about 1300, which served as the priory guest house. The north and south gable walls stand to their full height.

This unusual photograph shows the ruins of the guest house shrouded in ivy; the ivy has since been removed and the ruins now stand bare and impressive, especially in mist or when floodlit at night. By the time of the Dissolution, neglect had reduced the value of the buildings to just £125.

George Fossick's depiction of Boxgrove Priory Church and ruins. Barbara Willard wrote of the ruins: 'The place is heavy with the rejection of time but the priory church remains the parish church. This is half a blessing – enough is seen to make the loss of the rest more distressing.'

Barbara Willard wrote: 'Ruins stand among nettles and tall grasses in summertime and if they are melancholy they are equally impressive.' According to Cooke, the combination of neglect of rules, admission of unfit persons, luxury, gluttony, general worldliness and, worst of all, the admission of women into certain areas, made Boxgrove Priory's fall a certainty during the Dissolution. When the blow fell in 1537, Lord de la Warr stepped in to prevent the priory church being pulled down and was responsible for its conversion into the parish church.

The Winterton Arms in the hamlet of Crockerhill, near Boxgrove. This pub is over 200 years old and for many years it has been a popular watering hole for race-goers at nearby Goodwood.

SOUTH OF CHICHESTER

There are numerous communities to the south of Chichester, including Dell Quay, Hunston, Mundham, Runcton and Merston. Yet despite the number of villages, there is comparatively little of real historical interest to attract the photographer, and one suspects that these little villages were generally perceived as little more than places to be passed through on the journey between Chichester and the coast. Separated from the city itself by the A27 bypass, these villages have retained their rural nature and sense of identity, and it is therefore a pleasure to conclude this book with images of a more peaceful nature.

For many years Dell Quay served as Chichester's nearest accessible port, having replaced the old port of Appledram (also spelt Apuldram) at the upper end of Chichester harbour in the seventeenth century. The village also boasts the popular Anchor Inn, pictured above on a sunny day in the mid-1950s. The picture on the left depicts the sun setting over Chichester harbour near Dell Quay. This is the closest that Chichester harbour gets to the city itself, so it was natural that, following Chichester's flood disaster in January 1994, millions of gallons of water were pumped into the sea near here. Eighteen months later, there was talk of hosepipe bans. . . .

These attractive old thatched cottages stood in Runcton, now separated from Chichester by the A27 bypass. Runcton itself was also graced with a medieval priory.

The old church at Hunston before it was demolished in 1885. By October of the same year a new church had been put in its place. Ian Nairn and Nikolaus Pevsner wrote of the new church: 'There are very few Sussex churches for which absolutely nothing can be said. Alas, this is one of them.'

The Chichester Canal at Hunston. Although it may not have an interesting church, Hunston does boast an impressive waterway! Commercial usage of the canal ceased in 1934. This was hardly surprising in view of the new road bridge which presented an impenetrable obstacle to eastbound canal craft.

The Manor House at Hunston. This rather austere-looking building dates from between 1600 and 1680, although the stone angle dressings to the lower storey are probably medieval. At one time the house was surrounded by a moat.

Hunston windmill, also known as Kipson Bank Mill. Owned by Hodsons, the millers, between 1865 and 1915, this black smock-mill contained a unique ten-sided base 23 ft across. Constructed originally in the early eighteenth century, the ten-sided mill was built of brick and cement and tarred on the outside. After many years of idleness it was pulled down in 1919.

Happy members of a tennis party, photographed in the 1920s. Seated on the right is Brian Tyler, who was a prominent architect in Chichester at that time.

This cricket team at Hunston, pictured in about 1895, was largely made up of local farmers, and they played on the cricket field on Hunston Common, by Brimfast Lane. It is not easy to tell the difference between team members and spectators, but I should be surprised if the two men seated on the left made many runs! Mr Jupp of Hoe Farm is fourth from the left in the back row. Hoe Farm was a halt on the old Selsey Tramway, which began running between Chichester and Selsey in 1897.

An impromptu orchestra photographed in a garden in North Mundham, *c.* 1905. Among those present are C.A. Hodson, C. Shrubb, S. Sanders, H. Binsted and the Revd J.C.B. Fletcher.

'Your Country Needs You' . . . the Sussex Reserves pictured shortly before the First World War.